A PRIMER ON
WORSHIP
AND
REFORMATION

RECOVERING THE HIGH CHURCH PURITAN

DOUGLAS WILSON

canonpress
Moscow, Idaho

Published by Canon Press
P.O. Box 8729, Moscow, ID 83843
800.488.2034 | www.canonpress.com

Douglas Wilson, *A Primer on Worship and Reformation:
Recovering the High Church Puritan*
Copyright © 2008, Douglas Wilson.
Cover design by Rachel Hoffmann.
Printed in the United States of America.

Scripture taken from the King James Version, unless otherwise noted. All emphases are the author's.

Library of Congress Cataloging-in-Publication Data

Wilson, Douglas, 1953-
  A primer on worship and reformation : recovering the high church Puritan
/ Douglas Wilson.
      p. cm.
  ISBN-13: 978-1-59128-061-3 (pbk.)
  ISBN-10: 1-59128-061-3 (pbk.)
  1. Public worship--Reformed Church. I. Title.
  BX9427.W55 2008
  264'.042--dc22
                        2008027178

08 09 10 11 12 13   10 9 8 7 6 5 4 3 2 1

CONTENTS

INTRODUCTION

In conservative Reformed circles, a small but promising liturgical movement now appears to be underway. This movement
is seeking to recover a practical understanding of the centrality
and potency of godly worship—a worship that self-consciously
renews covenant with God on a weekly basis. This small book
represents an introductory effort to point out the need for such
reformation, to discuss the nature of it, and then provide a de-
scription of what some of the fruit might look like.

The need for such a reformation is apparent when we look
at the various cultural indicators of what defines an evangelical believer in America today. Those who surround themselves
with Jesus junk obtained at their local holy hardware store feel
free to do so because of how they worship God. This state of
affairs did not befall us out of a clear, blue sky—it has historical
antecedents. By and large, this is thanks to the rise of religious
individualism over the last several centuries and the subsequent
democratization of the Faith. But of course, an ever-present
temptation is to fight fire with fire, and so conservatives have
to be warned to actually *conserve* something. We need to strive
for reformation in the Church without introducing additional

schismatic incentives. This will lead naturally to a discussion of our (apparently) oxymoronic subtitle. What, exactly, is a high church Puritan?

High church Puritan thinking begins with the authority of the Word of God, and one of the first things we are told in Scripture is that God has established enmity between the seed of the woman and the seed of the serpent. An understanding of this enmity, this antithesis, must undergird all that we do. This affects how we present ourselves in evangelism to the unbelieving world, and it affects how and why we gather in worship as the people of God. Covenant renewal is the point of all worship, but this worship also has some constituent elements that need to be reconsidered in the light of what the entire worship service actually is. And so we will consider hermeneutics and the preaching of the Word, just as we will consider the role of the sacraments in a reformation of worship. Music is another area of worship where our contemporary trivialization of holy things is most apparent, and so we will note the central role the Psalms must play in any reformation of worship. The cumulative effect of all of this is an overflow of gladness and joy, and so we briefly touch on feasting and the Lord's Day. Worship is warfare, but we are to conduct this warfare in a certain way. And last, we will embrace the importance of including and training our children in this duty of covenant renewal worship. Only in this way will what we undertake be reformational in any important sense. Without our children loving and understanding these things more than we do, all this talk of covenant renewal will be just a Reformed version of those fads or fashions that we see so frequently in the church renewal guru books—with titles like *Unleashing the Vibrant Church,* or *Vibrating the Unleashed Church.* Something like that. Which leads to our first consideration.

1

THEY'LL KNOW WE ARE CHRISTIANS BY OUR SCHLOCK

The Church in our nation is in a bad way. This comment is not directed at our moribund quadrant—the ever-relevant liberals dozing off irrelevantly in their ecumenical corner—but rather at the vibrant and active section that we call modern evangelicalism. Now of course there isn't a problem with activity per se, but in the conservative and evangelical wing of the Church, vibrancy and activity always seem to cluster around cash registers.

This is not written with a sense of ironic detachment; we understand ourselves to be covenantally united with the modern evangelical church. We do not just attack these corruptions; we also confess them. Because we have confessed them, and continue to confess them, we do not hesitate to call for the *thorough* reform of the contemporary Church, root and branch. And in order to avoid spiritual confusion, this reform must concern itself first and last with the reform of the worship of God.

> Seeing that many glory after the flesh, I will glory also.
> For ye suffer fools gladly, seeing ye yourselves are wise.

> For ye suffer, if a man bring you into bondage, if a man devour you, if a man take of you, if a man exalt himself, if a man smite you on the face. I speak as concerning reproach, as though we had been weak. Howbeit whereinsoever any is bold, (I speak foolishly,) I am bold also. (2 Cor. 11:18–21)

In this passage, Paul is rebuking the Corinthians for the tolerance that they show to fools—the reference being to the fools who oppress them in the name of bringing them the Word of God. Such ministers are glory hounds, but it is a glorying after the flesh. Two can play this game, Paul says, and so he will glory also. Paul sarcastically notes that the Corinthians are *so* wise, and this wisdom of theirs is the basis for them "suffering fools gladly." He says that they will tolerate and put up with men who exploit them—but are in effect intolerant of true shepherds. As the people of God, we are being abused by the leadership of the modern evangelical movement—by this I mean the men standing behind the cash registers—and we cravenly submit. We know the taste of boot polish.

We consequently need to conduct an *inventory of our relics*. This phrase is taken from a pamphlet written by John Calvin, the full title of which was *An Admonition Showing the Advantages Which Christendom Might Derive from an Inventory of Relics*. Writing in the midst of a great Reformation of the Church, Calvin pointed out the church's level of degradation and superstition by noting that if an inventory were actually taken, they would discover that every apostle had more than four bodies, and every saint two or three. Although he didn't put it this way, it is hard to take any view seriously when it would result in enough pieces of the Virgin Mary's veil to make a tent for Barnum and Bailey.

But the point of this is inspiration, not duplication. It is far too easy to preach against the sins of others, or attempt to bring about a Reformation that was necessary for another era.

We do need a Reformation in our day, but this means we need to be forgiven for *our* sins. And this means, in its turn, that we must repent of *our* sins. But how will we hear without a preacher? And how will they turn red and embarrassed without a satirist?

Making all necessary adjustments for the changes in time and place, the modern evangelical Church, eyes fat as grease, bastion of born againism, is fully as corrupt as the Church prior to the Reformation. And this is not a back-handed way of praising the Church prior to the Reformation. When a people have given themselves over to a lie, the scriptural pattern is for God to give them over to more lies, so that they might learn to eat their own cooking. The further into the delusion we go, the starker the evidence of such delusion is, and the more difficult it is to get anyone to see what has actually happened. And on those occasions when someone will admit that there are "excesses" out there, it is still glibly assumed that these excesses are scattered around the periphery of modern evangelicalism. And thus, we heal the wound lightly, saying peace, peace, when there is no peace. This idolatry is right at the heart of our identity as modern evangelicals. We have sold out the faith for a buck. The one thing in our favor is that we made a bigger profit than Judas did. And, unlike Judas, we *keep* what we get.

Like the ancient Corinthians, modern evangelicalism *suffers fools gladly.* The point is not that every individual in the contemporary Church is a scoundrel. The point is that there are many scoundrels, doing very well, thank you, and the rest of us put up with them. This is our sin: *we suffer fools gladly.* And when anyone dares to rebuke the folly, revealing it for what it actually is, *then* we rouse ourselves to rebuke the one who dares to do this thing. Let someone write a trivial and inane novel about holy things, a novel bad enough to make your back teeth ache, and yet everyone sits there as solemn as a judge. I recall picking up a novel one time in a Christian book store and turned to the passage where Jesus was breaking up with his girl friend (I think her name was Tara) because he had to go off and do the Messiah thing. Let someone write a series of novels about the Apocalypse that has the depth of a painted backdrop in a junior high play, and the modern evangelical world beats a path to their door. Let someone else write *The Vending Machine of Jabez* and sell millions of copies—is the result anything like anguish and repentance? Not a bit of it—we are too busy turning this opportunity around. There are *Vending Machine* bars of soap to be manufactured and sold! Anyone who expresses doubts about this probably doesn't have a zeal to win the lost. Probably doesn't buy Testamints® to share with unbelieving friends either.

The Church, when compromised, always tends to adapt itself to the surrounding and prevailing idolatry. When surrounded with the baals of Canaan, the Israelites did not chase after Greek gods. And in the American pantheon, one of the central gods is Mammon. Consequently, the compromised Church of our day bows and scrapes before the altar of this Mammon—and does so while calling the energy expended in all this shuffling a form of evangelism. "In the beginning was the logo, and the logo was with Mammon, and the logo was Mammon. And the people gathered and said they would obey all the words of this law."

We are not attacking a trifle. Christian retailing is a four *billion* dollar a year industry. This is no peripheral thing; in the pursuit of Mammon, modern evangelicals are *ardent* disciples. Like one famous grafter of Tammany Hall, our motto is "I seen my opportunities and I took 'em." The results are a grotesque parody of biblical Christianity. Let's begin with logo imitation. *Christ Supreme* instead of *Krispy Kreme*. *Fruit of the Spirit* instead of *Fruit of the Loom*. *J. Christ* in for *J. Crew*. We have *Christ the King* instead of *Calvin Klein*. This leads us to conclude that all our taste is in our mouth. Speaking of mouths, we have Bible Bars featuring the seven foods listed in Deuteronomy 8:8. You can get a "Depend Upon Christ the King" rubber ducky. Perhaps you want to purchase some "Satan Stomper" socks. If you want, you can purchase a self-help volume entitled *How to Live Through a Bad Day: Seven Powerful Insights from Christ's Words on the Cross.* Some of this would make a cat laugh. Little wonder that Stephen Bates, writing about this kind of thing in the *Weekly Standard,* found it a bit "unsettling." But not everyone is unsettled. "Arlo Pignotti of *godisdead.com,* for instance, entertains atheist conventions with his collection of Bible action figures and other 'holy paraphernalia.'" Bates was not surprised that an atheist would mock this pious tomfoolery. He *was* surprised however to find that some "equally pointed jabs" came from believing Christians. Several of the jabs he mentioned included the Canon publications of *The Mantra of Jabez* by Douglas Jones and *Right Behind* by Nathan Wilson. In effect, this is how far we have fallen. A sympathetic cultural observer was surprised to find that there might be some Christians who objected to blasphemy. These are curious times we live in. At least the money changers in the Temple were selling animals that the law required to be sacrificed. We modern evangelicals set up shop in the Temple in order to sell blasphemous T-shirts, concerning which Moses said nothing at all. Why not have a post-it note left on the cross, with Jesus dashing off a message thereon about how He has gone off to see His dad? "Be back soon!" Why would any Christian object to this? Oh, I don't know. Fear of God maybe.

And then there are the Veggie Tales. What is the issue here? That would become abundantly clear if someone seriously suggested a Veggie Tales version of *Beowulf,* or *Lord of the Rings,* or *Prince Caspian.* Modern evangelicals are reverent of everything *except* their religion. Just try to picture Aragorn as a cucumber. What does that do to the ethos of the thing? Or imagine Aslan as a beet. "We couldn't do that! It would wreck the *story!*" I see. Apparently, as far as modern evangelicals are concerned, the Bible doesn't have a story to wreck. If misguided evangelicals were to try to bridge current tensions by making a Veggie Tales version of the Koran, they would all now be in hiding because of the *fatwa* declared against them. In short, the Muslims would respond with outrage over what had been perpetrated on their holy book. But we are not outraged for two reasons—first, we are clueless, and second, we did it to ourselves.

Folks defend Veggie Tales because they inculcate biblical moral values—but such values apart from reverence for *who God is* are nothing but hollow moralism. And moralism is always morally impotent. The fear of the Lord is the beginning of wisdom, including all moral wisdom, and that fear cannot be effectually made obsolete by means of cute cartoon characters.

In addition, modern evangelicals have a ravenous hunger to be hipper than thou. They have a deep and covetous *hunger to be cool*—and so we have bestselling authors, Grammy award winners, trademark lawyers, Designer Bibles with Study Notes for just about everybody, rock bands with guys filled with middle-class white guy angst, earrings, and tattoos to match, rock bands with Christian women as sexy as it gets, for that special born-again T & A market niche, and onward into the fog. The biblical name for all this is *worldliness*. And to paraphrase the late P.T. Barnum, there is a sucker born again every minute.

There are only three options, which reduce actually to only two. One is to attack the folly. The weapons may vary—sermons, satire, conversation, books like this one, or prayer—but the target must always be to topple the idols. The other two options amount to just one. Join in with the wickedness, or simply suffer it gladly.

Now what does all this have to do with worship, or the reformation of worship? All cultures have a *cultus* at the center. The center of every culture *is its worship*. There is no such thing as a religion-less culture, and the same is true of all subcultures. Not surprisingly, the modern evangelical flotsam and jetsam at your local Jesus Junk Store is what we find floating on the surface after the shipwreck of reverent worship. In short, if you look at what passes for worship in most modern evangeli-cal churches today, you cannot be a bit surprised at what the people who worship in that way buy when they go out the next day to their local Bible and Bauble Book Shop.

Modern cheesiness in worship is now approaching its ze-nith. Recently, my wife and I were in another city on vacation on the Lord's Day, and so we sought out a place for worship. We picked a church that seemed (somewhat) safe by its name, and joined them to worship our God together. To make a long story short, the high point of the singing portion of the ser-vice was when the song leader had everyone put one arm out straight in front, with the other hand behind the head, in order that all the congregants might spin about in place, spritzing like lawn sprinklers. "Who says that church isn't *fun!*" cried one of the song leaders in a moment of religious fervor. When it comes to devotion, Thomas à Kempis got nothing on us.

The great argument advanced today in favor of such seeker sensitive worship is that we have to present the gospel to to-day's unbeliever in a way that is relevant to him. But the word *relevance,* though it has a fine dictionary definition, really has to be understood as the battle cry of modern unbelief. This is not because the word itself is objectionable, but because liberals and their modern evangelical cousins have freighted it with a hidden system of weights and measures—in which the world, *and not Scripture,* determines the content of our faith and prac-tice.

There are at least two kinds of irrelevance. One is the ir-relevance of offering a bicycle to an oyster. But there is another kind of irrelevance entirely, and that is the practice of setting forth the gospel of light and righteousness to those who love their darkness and iniquity. We are *commanded* to be irrelevant in this second sense. We are called to worship God in a way that is pleasing to Him, and to which unbelievers will be attracted *only if God moves them in a sovereign and mysterious way.*

13

In the modern world, worship that is pleasing to God will stand out as unusual, but *not* because it emphasizes external forms and liturgy while pop evangelical worship does not. It would be more accurate to say that all such external forms are inescapable—meaning that everyone does them. It just looks like "liturgical churches" are emphasizing them more because the forms are so different from our prevailing culture. The typical modern evangelical church also has music, worship, feasts, sabbaths, and church buildings. But the music is that of the Beach Boys ("Crown, crown, I get a crown"), worship modeled after night clubs and television shows, feasts on secular occasions, sabbaths in honor of new gods (Martin Luther King, Jr.), and church buildings that look like the mall.

The traditional and historic forms stand out, but not because Old Testament physical forms are intruding into a New Testament "spiritual" era. Rather, physical expressions of one inward faith differ from other physical expressions of other inward faiths. The reason the contemporary expression is not noticed is because everything about it is so commonplace. The *forms* of contemporary worship are not hard to see because they are spiritual; they are hard to see because they have thoroughly taken on the color of their surroundings. While it is true that angels are hard to see, so are chameleons.

To reapply the words of Henry Van Til, all cultures, *including all ecclesiastical cultures,* are the externalization of a religion. The only question to ask and answer is—what religion? Contemporary forms of worship express a religion. Which one? Historic liturgies express a religion. Which one? And is it the same one? This brings us back to our initial discussion of the current evangelical bedlam. Jesus said to judge by the fruit.

Of course, anti-contemporary worship forms do not carry any potency in the forms themselves. One cannot reform an ecclesiastical culture from the outside in, even if the outside is called "God-centered worship." We know that you cannot wash the outside of the cup and thereby make the inside clean.

Love is measurement of all things spiritual. But the Bible teach-es that love is defined by our behavior in the world of matter. I have encountered those who tell us that the one thing needful is for us to emphasize love, but they do it in markedly unloving ways ("Calvinists aren't loving. *Jerks.*"). Some might say this divide is the result of some glorifying doctrine while others em-phasize love. But from where I sit, the New Testament talks about Christians glorying in their doctrine and consequently loving one another with their bodies and all their stuff.

Those who want to live this way seek to emphasize love as shown in obedience to God's commandments—God's com-mandments with regard to our hands, our feet, our tongues, and our lives. And of course, it must all *begin* in the heart. "[I]f there be any other commandment, it is briefly comprehended in this saying, namely, Thou shalt love thy neighbour as thy-self. Love worketh no ill to his neighbour: therefore love is the fulfilling of the law" (Rom. 13:9–10). And of course, "For this is the love of God, that we keep his commandments: and his commandments are not grievous" (1 Jn. 5:3). Another way of saying this is that we want our love to take incarnational forms. We do not just want to *say* that love is important, but we also want to unload moving vans, prepare meals for the bedridden, prepare feasts to invite people to, build buildings that glorify God, rest on the Lord's Day so that we do not grind those we love into soul-weariness, and so forth, more and more.

The typological value of all such "external" things in the Old Testament *is* fulfilled in Christ. But it is not true to say that the value of a drink is done away: a glass of cold water given in the Savior's name will still be remembered at the last day (Mt. 10:42). We still need food, drink, and rest, and we need them in Christ. The key is what Paul points to—righteousness, peace, and joy in the Holy Ghost. Reformational Christians do exhibit these things, and in the meantime, those who disparage the world of incarnational obedience emphasize "righteousness, peace, and joy," in the abstract, on paper and in name. Yet their lives are still unhappy, critical, and resentful. Hollow theology cannot result in full lives.

So we are not emphasizing one culture in order to counteract another. We are emphasizing a potent Christian faith which will take an incarnational form quite distinct from the incarnational form taken by alien faiths and compromised faiths. In short, we are emphasizing the *gospel* without all the attached gnostic inhibitors which the modern evangelical church applies. A gnostic inhibitor is the teaching that love is a matter of the heart—period. The biblical gospel brings a potent love that *begins* in the heart, and ends at the fingertips. Those fingertips may be making a salad, caressing a wife, or laying masonry in the cloister, but they must glorify God in Christ through all that they do.

This is an important part of our sanctification. It is not, however, the means of our sanctification, but rather the stuff of our sanctification. The Holy Spirit is the one who leads us into these things. A table will not bring us to Christ, but Christ most certainly brings us to a table.

— 2

HOW WE GOT HERE

A great deal of trouble is contained in the suffix *-ism*. There is nothing wrong with piety, for example, but piet*ism* has caused no end of grief. And the Christian faith exalts the importance of the individual—we go to heaven or hell by ones—but individual*ism* is the result of taking each individual, not as a man or woman created in the image of God, but rather as a self-contained epistemology.

This very modern process started in earnest with Descartes, who sought to ground ultimate certainty in *self*. Radical doubt, he said, can get to everything except the fact that I am doubting. And so Descartes tried to build epistemic certainty on the foundation of a man-centered starting point. As the leaven worked its way through Christendom, religious forms of this man-centered mentality began to pervade the Church. In the "liberal" sections of the Church, it took the form of exalting the intellect of man over the Scriptures. In the "conservative" sections of the Church, it took the form of exalting personal conversion experiences over the revelation of God. The peculiar American form of this became noticeable by the First Great Awakening in the mid-eighteenth century. By the Second Great

Awakening, it had metastasized in the excitements presided over by men like Finney.

The result is that we now have to deal with a vice that we are very proud of—our individualism. Such virtues are the hardest things in the world to repent of. Jesus taught that quisling tax collectors and prostitutes were closer to the kingdom of heaven because they *knew* they had a problem. But the Pharisees, full of hot air which they mistook for the Spirit of God, were confident of their own righteousness. Since they were in fact unrighteous, this confidence was obviously misplaced.

In the conservative church today, the sin that has us by the throat is individualism. And the reason it has us by the throat is that we see it as a virtue—the rugged individualism that made America great. There are many forms of individualism, but the one thing they all have in common is the refusal to submit to lawful authority. Harmony in the church is possible only so long as everyone agrees. But as soon as disagreement arises, submission becomes impossible for the individualist. But of course, true submission at a particular point is actually impossible for the individual *unless* there is disagreement. If a husband were to ask his wife to put on her best red dress so that they could go out to a fancy restaurant, she would not say, "Honey . . . I submit." The place were submission is tested is always at the point of significant disagreement.

When we think we have only two options—complete agreement or open defiance—we have left out the greenhouse where true humility grows. That greenhouse is a place of cheerful compliance with a legitimate authority that is believed to be mistaken. And individualistic objections crowd into our minds. But what if a husband commands his wife to commit adultery, what then? Well, she respectfully and submissively disobeys. But *that* is not the problem we normally face. What if the elders excommunicate the godliest person in the church? Well, that happens sometimes too, but such exceptions are not where the action is. The kingdom of God grows because of all the controversies and splits that *don't* happen because the saints were busy submitting to one another in the bond of peace. If we are constantly on guard against the monstrous tyranny, we will never learn to humble ourselves when we differ in ordinary things. And ironically, because we have not learned humility before God, we are *more* susceptible to the tyranny if and when it happens.

Every individualist has his very own sword to fall on. It might be birth control, elder qualifications, church government, education methods, pietistic scruples, or just personal animosities. When the moment of crisis comes, the church has apparently just "compromised" in the eyes of the individualist, and this amounts to a declaration of ecclesiastical war. In Presbyterian churches, somebody brings charges, and the elders get the bureaucratic "church discipline trial machine" oiled and lubed. In Baptist churches, people start lobbying for the congregational meeting where the church split will happen. In both cases, people start preparing themselves to ignore what the Scriptures teach about mutual submission. Presbyterians adjudicate every dog fight up to the General Assembly, followed by a church split, while the Baptists are far more efficient and have the church split right away, and with far less paperwork.

The worst species of individualism is the pietistic strain. Individualists on governmental or social issues can sometimes be made to see that there is a deeper right than being right about whatever their issue is. But because pietists have staked out the ultimate high ground—communion with God, walking with Jesus, and mystic fellowship with the Holy Spirit—their issue always trumps all others. To this kind of super-spirituality, we should respond the same way that Luther did to *his* enthusiast opponents. He did not care if they had swallowed the Holy Ghost, feathers and all.

This pietistic individualism always leads directly to impiety. But the impiety is frequently *invisible* impiety because the paradigmatic assumptions about what is occurring are so strong. I have seen very pious people do and say some awful things, and all with a serene lack of awareness that they were flatly disobeying what God said to do in His Word. This usually results in setting up false standards of holiness—you must not drink alcohol, you must witness every day, you must separate from churches on the slightest provocation, and you must dumb down worship so that a non-Christian will feel comfortable there.

It also results in a jaundiced and backward view of the world. Doctrine and love cannot be separated, and when people try, it is to topple one and make an idol of the other. But of course, we always lose the very thing we idolize. This is why the besetting sin of doctrinalists is that of *irrationalism.* Read through transcripts of church trials from staunchly doctrinal churches, and you find yourself at the Mad Hatter's Tea Party. But spend any time at all with "all you need is love" Christians, and you will discover just how nasty they can be. This is because their highest virtue (evaluated individualistically, of course) is piety. Who could be against that? And who can prove them wrong about themselves?

We get messages from outside our hearts—which we as sinners desperately need—through submission. We submit to God and His authoritative and infallible Scripture. We submit to God and His authoritative and fallible Church. We submit to God and the fallible familial authorities He has placed in our lives. We submit to God and to the fallible and frequently unrighteous civil authority He has established over us. When we are in positions of authority in any of these settings, we teach the people under us how to submit by demonstrating it for them, living it out, as we submit to those above us. And in so doing, we learn wisdom.

This is important to master because we are calling for *reformation.* In doing this, we do not simply want to hoist a different flag to see who salutes. A true reformation has to be undertaken in a different *manner.* In working for reformation, we need to avoid a false dilemma. Some peaceable souls call for unity, but they believe the cost of unity is compromise, and it is cost they are willing to pay. Warlike conservatives call for truth, but they believe the cost of truth is always separation and disunity—which they too are willing to pay. This is a false choice.

We have to fight for reformation without schism. Decades ago, when the fundamentalists attacked Billy Graham for his willingness to share his platform with theological liberals, it was easy to dismiss their concerns at that time with a roll of the eyes. At the time, modern evangelicalism still had a doctrinal backbone, and it was possible to see the whole effort as a form of strategic evangelism. But since that time, in what he is willing to bless, not only has Billy Graham capitulated both to Roman Catholicism *and* liberalism, it is also clear he has become a liberal himself. Far from winning liberals with the gospel, the liberals tragically won him. And so, as far as this issue goes, the fundamentalists were demonstrably right.

But underneath the controversy was another issue, and in this matter the fundamentalists were as compromised as Billy Graham was and were equal contributors to the problem. Because American evangelicals (and fundamentalists) tend to believe that the invisible church is visible to *them,* this means that to include someone as a member of the church is tantamount to a declaration of peace and harmony. Conservatives see that the Christian faith and liberalism are two antithetical faiths in principle, and so they exclude liberals. The whole thing is so simple; those guys can't be Christians. Evangelical moderates see that schism is distressing, and so they raise the welcoming glass to just about anyone, and try to promote a general glow of bonhomie. The conservative wants standards and no unity. The moderate wants unity and no standards. The biblical requirement is to demand both unity and standards, backing up the demand by fighting for both. So the covenantal alternative is to accept these liberal gentlemen as fellow Christians, and then fight them to the death.

Take the example of marriage. A theological liberal in a mainstream denomination should be considered *covenantally* a Christian, even though he denies the virgin birth, the substitutionary death of Christ, the resurrection, and the final judgment. He is a Christian in just the same way that an adulterous husband is a husband. The unfaithful man remains a husband—even though he has slept with Suzy, Sally, Shirley, et al. The fact such a man is a husband compounds his guilt; it does not lessen it in any way. If we knew that a man was promiscuous, and then found out he was married, we wouldn't say, "Well, at *least* he's married!" His covenant vows make his sin worse. When a single man sleeps around, his sin is great. When an infidel says that God didn't create the world, his sin is great. When a married man is sexually treacherous, his sin is multiplied many times over. And when a liberal bishop says that Christ was merely a man, he is more than wrong. He is treacherous, and an antichrist. *But he does belong to that which he betrays.* Judas was this kind of bishop (Acts 1:20).

So throughout the traditional debate over ecumenical issues, a false assumption has plagued us. One side knows we must fight this or that heretical error, and so we say those who are guilty of the error are not Christians in any way. Those who know they are Christians in some way assume that we should therefore not fight with them. But we must fight them *especially* because they bear the name of Christ. What does a faithful shepherd do with a savage wolf? He fights. And where do savage wolves appear? "For I know this, that after my departing shall grievous wolves enter in *among you,* not sparing the flock. Also *of your own selves* shall men arise, speaking perverse things, to draw away disciples after them" (Acts 20:29–30). So, are these men in the covenant? Of course they are, which is why they are so dangerous.

If we learn this, we will learn to fight without being schismatic in attitude. Because we conservatives think this way, we have come to divide almost as a matter of course. And this becomes (soon enough) the way we handle disagreements among fellow conservatives—our spirits have become narrow and truncated. But in a fight a man needs a large heart and a narrow sword. We have jumbled everything, and now have narrow hearts, and our swords are clumsily made from two by fours. We need to recover—soon—the ideal of the Puritan cavalier.

American Christians only know one method of fighting, which is to divide and run off to yet another splinter denomination, the Presbytery of the True Flame. This, to use the military parlance, is called *retreating*. Moderates fraternize with evil covenant members and call it unity. A better term would be *betrayal*. Conservatives run from evil covenant members and call it purity. A better term would be *rout*. Of course, as we learn to apply all this, it will not be long before the local liberal ministerial association writes you a polite letter that indicates, ahem, that perhaps you might be able to find another association more to your liking. We cannot do what we cannot do. But something we can do is alter our language. We can stop talking as though we can see into hearts. We can stop acting as though Christ's standards for fighting are optional. We can stop acting like the hireling, who doesn't care about the sheep.

— 3

HIGH CHURCH PURITANS

And this brings us to a defense of our name for all this. The original Puritans—Elizabethans—wanted to cleanse the Church of England of its remaining papal corruptions. Henry had separated from Rome for the sake of his divorce, but the Church of England remained largely Catholic without a pope. Or, rather, Henry was now functionally pope. While the Puritans were happy about the break from Rome, there was still a long way to go.

Because they wanted to purify the church, they were abusively called Puritans and the name stuck. Unfortunately, the name stuck to everything. Consequently, the word *Puritan* is now used, and misused, in applications that are as wide-ranging as they are misleading. It can mean almost anything. Some uses are just a few shades off, while other applications are almost the reverse of the original historic meaning. H.L. Mencken used it as one of his favorite terms of abuse for the wowsers who were in his day afflicting the Republic. When talking about the settlement of New England, people routinely confuse the Puritans with the Pilgrims. Others think that *puritanical* describes those who are sexually repressed, which is about 180 degrees from the original application. Still others think of the Cromwellian revolution in England as being Puritan from stem to stern. But of course that revolution was a century after the first Puritans, and excluded from its ranks the true heirs of the original movement. The roundheads had little in common with the original Puritans.

And so I want to use the word in its original sense—one who has a deep desire to purify the Church, but who has no intention of voluntarily separating from his church if he doesn't get his way immediately. While retaining his covenantal connection to the Church, he conducts a glad warfare for the sake of Christ's honor wherever that honor might be challenged. Because the word by itself has been so badly handled, it is impossible to say *Puritan* without qualifications and still have any hope of being understood. And so I say *high church Puritan.* Because he is *high church,* he does not behave like a schismatic, separatist, independent, or individualist. He has a high view of the covenant, and of our corporate identity with one another. Because he is a *Puritan,* he intends to be a theological cavalier, and he fights for the integrity of obedience. He does not do this as some gloomy caricature, sitting in the back pews lamenting the regrettable apostasies up front. As C.S. Lewis noted, "It follows that nearly every association which now clings to the word *puritan* has to be eliminated when we are thinking of the early Protestants. Whatever they were, they were not sour, gloomy, or severe; nor did their enemies bring any such charge against them." Of such high church Puritanism let it be said, once again, that it was not "too grim, but too glad, to be true."[1]

This cannot be done without affirming *sola Scriptura*—the primacy of Scripture and the centrality of gospel within those Scriptures. At the beginning of our history, God said that there would be a standing enmity between the seed of the

[1] C.S. Lewis, *English Literature in the 16th Century* (Oxford: Clarendon Press, 1954), 34.

woman and the seed of the serpent. But this was not enmity for enmity's sake—rather, it was enmity for salvation's sake. The seed of the woman would come to crush the serpent's head, and in that conquest we would find our salvation.

There are two elements here, which we sum up with the word *antithesis:* authority and kindness. First, authority. God's Word, by definition, comes to us as an absolute. The serpent had tempted Eve by getting her to entertain doubts about the Word of God. ("Did God *really* say . . . ") After the Fall, when God established the antithesis between the brood of vipers and the children of salvation, the division is clearly visible at this place. The two seeds are identified by their relation to His Word, by their response to it. Jesus said that His sheep hear His voice. Those who are the seed of the woman are characterized by their faith in what God has said, which is always sufficient for them. The offspring of the serpent are always looking for another, alien authority, and they always find it. They also seal their own damnation. God grants their request and sends leanness to their souls.

But this antithesis also includes covenant kindness. One side of the divide is left in sin and rebellion, while the other is brought out of that rebellion into the mercy of God in Christ. Not surprisingly, those who are left behind in sin concoct their own gospels, their own flattering conceits. They are hostile to every form of holiness. Those who hear the Word of God rightly, however, do not just acknowledge its authority, but they also receive its kindness with joy, gladness, and simplicity of heart. They hate every form of ingratitude.

As we seek the reformation of the Church, therefore, our only infallible and ultimate standard must be *tota et sola Scriptura,* all of Scripture and only Scripture. When we challenge abuses in the Church, and we are asked for our standard, that standard is the Word of God. We are biblical absolutists. This does not mean that we are hostile to heritage or tradition— all churches have traditions—but it does mean that we insist that such traditions be subordinated to the ongoing authority of Scripture. We want to purify the Church. We are Puritans. *By what standard* do we want to purify the Church? The answer is Scripture.

But we do not just distrust the corruptions of other people "out there." We also distrust our own fevered brains. We believe that the Church has had enough self-appointed zealots, two-bit prophets, and hot gospelers. We know that we need accountability as well, an accountability that functions in real time, on the ground. We therefore need to have a high view of the Church, which is the pillar and ground of the truth. The Church is the community of those who are being saved together as God builds us up into a perfect man. As this process continues, to whom do we submit as we carry on the work of reformation? "Obey them that have the rule over you, and submit yourselves" (Heb. 13:17). The answer is the Church. Always beware the reformer who doesn't need ongoing reformation in himself. And so we are *high church* Puritans.

4

THE REFORMATION OF WORSHIP AND CULTURAL EVANGELISM

Such things cannot be done in a corner. As the worship of God in the Church is put right, it will have a dramatic impact on the unbelieving world outside. Just as our current shenanigans are comforting to them in their disobedience, so will our reformation be profoundly unsettling. When the Church abandons her disobedience, can the world be far behind?

It is important to begin this discussion with important qualifiers. Direct evangelism is of course necessary. Jesus Christ told His apostles to preach the gospel to every creature (Mk. 16:15). The marching orders of the Christian church, found in the Great Commission, require the Church to disciple the nations, baptize them, and teach them obedience to everything Christ required, which would of course include this last command (Mt. 28:18–20). The Great Commission is therefore self-perpetuating. The duty of world evangelism is therefore an obligation that rests upon the Church in each generation. And local churches are responsible for the evangelization of their communities. So much is obvious to every careful reader of the New Testament.

But if we compare a classical Protestant approach to this task with that of modern evangelicalism, we begin to differ in our shared commitment to this central principle. The differences between us become apparent at the practical level—what *tactics* should be employed in this effort? We agree that the gospel must be taken to the world, agreeing that the gospel must be preached "to every creature." But in contemporary evangelicalism there is a widespread assumption that this must be done by the following means: each individual Christian must acknowledge that his personal walk with God rests upon certain foundation stones—obvious things like prayer and Bible-reading, but also some not so obvious things like "witnessing daily."

Average Christians, as they are first discipled, are routinely taught that being a faithful Christian means telling someone about Christ every day. And of course, as young people are taught the pattern (this usually happens in college), some who are naturally gifted and outgoing do very well at it. They take to it. But others, and their number is great, have no desire *at all* to go up and down the hallways of the dormitories, knocking on doors and asking people to take a spiritual survey. But it is their spiritual duty, or so they have been taught, and so they sweat bullets, and do it anyway.

After they graduate, they enter another phase of their lives, one where there is a lot less free time, and where witnessing opportunities are not so abundant. With a strange mixture of gratitude and guilt, they stop telling people about Jesus every day. The guilt is stirred up occasionally by a missions speaker at church, but for the most part, they make their peace with that guilt. This compromise means the evangelistic zeal of the *entire* Church has been wounded. This is not because one individual has stopped sharing his faith daily, but rather because he was forced into sharing it in the first place on false pretenses. And this produces a bad reaction, and evangelism ceases to be important.

Of course, every Christian should be prepared to answer questions when non-believers ask them. We should (all of us) know what we believe, and why. We should (all of us) live in a manner that provokes the occasional question about *how* we believe. Peter is explicit on this point. "But sanctify the Lord God in your hearts: and be ready always to give an answer to every man that asketh you a reason of the hope that is in you with meekness and fear" (1 Pet. 3:15). But the work of an evangelist, which Paul exhorts Timothy to keep pursuing, is a demanding work (2 Tim. 4:5). A man should no more appoint himself to this task than with other callings in the church. Jesus Christ ascended into heaven and gave gifts to men—apostles, prophets, evangelists, and pastor/teachers (Eph. 4:11). If we were to adopt our common evangelistic approach in the other offices, the result would be governmental chaos. This giftedness bestowed by Christ is important, and reveals His authority. Not everyone is gifted in this way. Is everyone a teacher? No. Is everyone an evangelist? *No.* To insist that everyone share his faith daily in verbal, propositional form is to directly contradict what Paul taught us about the nature of body life. Not everyone in the body of Christ has the same function.

This is not to deny the centrality of the evangelistic mission to the life of the church. But say a man is going to a concert hall to play the piano—we should not consider him a failure if his kidneys are unable to play anything. They *support* him in what he is doing, but they do not do anything musical themselves. Without those kidneys, he would be off in a hospital, nowhere near a piano. But the kidneys still can't play. Attempts to make them try anyway are attempts that will necessarily harm the *man's* ability to play.

When David's men pursued the Amalekites who had sacked Ziklag, some of his troops were unable to keep up the pursuit, and so they stayed behind with the baggage. After the battle, certain churlish men with David wanted to withhold their portion of the spoil from them. But David said *no,* and made it an ordinance in Israel that they were all "in it together" (1 Sam. 30:24). The supply officer in the Pentagon, the cook on the submarine, the infantryman in the front lines—in it together, as each does his part. But suppose we made this rule: every cook has to fire at least one round at the enemy daily.

The task of evangelism is assigned to the *Church*. Many Christians are not gifted evangelistically. Such men should do an honest day's work (say, as an auto mechanic), be the best mechanic in town, attend church faithfully—assuming a faithful church that is engaged in the work of evangelism—and tithe to the work of the church. What shall we say about such men? We should say that they are *evangelical* men, whether or not they say a word. But if they excel in their vocational work, to the glory of God, the chances are good that they will periodically have to answer the kind of question Peter mentions.

Now this is not evangelistic abdication; rather, it is evangelistically potent. It is my contention that the biblical form of covenant renewal worship (outlined in the next section) should be self-consciously pursued as a form of cultural conquest. As we gather in the presence of the living God on the Lord's Day, He is pleased to use our right worship of Him as a battering ram to bring down all the citadels of unbelief in our communities. Just as the walls of Jericho fell before the worship and service of God, so unbelievers tremble when Christians gather in their communities to worship the living God rightly. Jesus promised us that the gates of Hades would not prevail against the Church. It is not often noted that the gates of Hades are not an offensive weapon. Hades is being besieged by the Church; *it is not the other way around.* We need to learn to see that biblical worship of God is a powerful battering ram, and each Lord's Day we have the privilege of taking another swing. Or, if we prefer, we might still want to continue gathering around with our insipid songs, dopey skits, and inspirational chats in order to pelt the gates of Hades with our wadded up kleenex.

— 5

COVENANT RENEWAL

As noted earlier, one of our besetting sins is individualism. This affects many areas of our lives, including how we see the Scriptures, and it is one of the foundational assumptions beneath most modern Bible reading. For example, Paul wrote the book of Ephesians to a *church,* but countless quiet times have taught us all to regard it as "a message for *me.*" "How should *I* behave today? What should *I* do tomorrow?" Instead of seeing Scripture as a most holy collection of the Church's covenant documents, we tend to see it as a grab-bag of inspirational quotes for personal victorious living. Every man for himself, and devil take the hindmost.

It is important to note that a corporate covenantal understanding of Scripture does not exclude personal faithfulness; rather, it requires it. It is not possible to make a good omelet with rotten eggs, and so nothing written here can be taken as a disparagement of personal faithfulness. But in contrast, an individualistic approach does not require corporate faithfulness. All the eggs in the world do not necessitate that someone make an omelet. In most cases, such individualism is sustained by a deliberate, cultivated low view of the institutional Church, and this is radically unscriptural.

This question of individualism is important whenever we discuss what the Bible teaches about the public worship of God. This is because we have trained ourselves to miss the setting in which many well-known verses appear. But when this corporate covenantal setting is taken into account, the testimony of Scripture is clear from beginning to end. God teaches us that public worship is *greatly* to be preferred over private spiritual exercises. "The LORD loveth the gates of Zion more than all the dwellings of Jacob. Glorious things are spoken of thee, O city of God" (Ps. 87:2–3). Every grateful heart wants God's name to be lifted up publicly—and the more public the better. "Declare his glory among the heathen, his wonders among *all* people" (Ps. 96:3). One of the most natural things for us to do as believers is congregate so that we might worship God *together.* "O come, let *us* worship and bow down: let *us* kneel before the LORD our maker" (Ps. 95:6). "O magnify the LORD with me, and *let us exalt his name together"* (Ps. 34:3).

Worship therefore belongs primarily in the congregation. "I will declare thy name unto my brethren: in the midst *of the congregation* will I praise thee . . . My praise shall be of thee *in the great congregation:* I will pay my vows before them that fear him" (Ps. 22:22, 25). Asaph struggled greatly in his private meditations—but when he finally went to the sanctuary, God taught him (Ps. 73:16–17).

After His conquest of the principalities and powers, Christ followed the ancient custom of triumphant kings and generals—*spargere missilia*—and He gave gifts to men. He gave these gifts so that His church would be built up into "a perfect man." In order to accomplish this very public goal He gave public officers, establishing them in the Church (Eph. 4:11–14). The early Christians were filled with the Holy Spirit when they were assembled *together* (Acts 4:31). The tabernacles of the Lord are always appealing to the forgiven (Ps. 84:1). A day in God's courts is better than a thousand elsewhere (Ps. 84:10), and yet God in His kindness permits us to assemble there every *seventh* day (Lev. 23:3). The man who believes this while trusting God is truly blessed (Ps. 84:12). What one thing does the godly man want? That he might *dwell* in the house of God (Ps. 27:4). This is no fossilized relic of the forms of worship in the Old Testament. The day will come, the prophet said, when the inhabitant of one city will drag his brother off to worship God—and "I will go also" (Zech. 8:20–21).

Christians have the enormous privilege of ascending into heaven in their worship on the Lord's Day. This consecration, this lifting up, is what happens when the call to worship is given. When John was in the Spirit on the Lord's Day (Rev. 1:10), he was caught up into the heavenly places. The same thing happens to us—on the first day of every week. "And the smoke of the incense, which came with the prayers of the saints, ascended up before God out of the angel's hand" (Rev. 8:4).

Paul tells the Ephesians that they were located in two places. The first was obvious—Ephesus (Eph. 1:1). But their second location is something he emphasizes strongly throughout the book. They are *in Christ,* who is in turn at the right hand of God the Father *in heaven.* According to Paul, we were co-crucified with Christ, co-resurrected, and co-enthroned "in heavenly places in Christ Jesus" (Eph. 2:5–6). We read these passages, but we individualize them. We go off to heaven in our private prayers and rarely wonder where everyone else is.

Why should we not forsake the gathering of ourselves *together* (Heb. 10:25)? Too often this verse is quoted as simply meaning that a man should "go to church." It means this, of course, but neglects the riches involved when we go to church with a scriptural heart and mind. This is really a command to not neglect going to *heaven* in worship. The preceding context makes this abundantly clear. We have boldness to enter the Holy of Holies in heaven (10:19). How holy must *that* sanctuary be? Because we have this boldness, let *us* draw near with true hearts (10:22). When do we do this? We draw near on the sabbath rest that remains for the people of God (4:9), which is to say, on the Lord's Day. God created the heavens and earth in six days, and He hallowed the seventh day as one of holy rest. No sufficient reason for changing the day can be found— short of a new heavens and a new earth, in which righteousness dwells. We have a new sabbath because we have a new creation; the old has passed away. And this is just what we find. Jesus Christ rested after His glorious work of re-creation, just as God had rested after the work of creation (4:10). This is why we still have a sabbath, and why we have the privilege of entering into a glorious heavenly rest.

In our public worship, we do not come to a mountain that can be touched (12:18), but we *do* come to a mountain, a heavenly Zion. What happens when a small group of saints gathers in a clapboard community church somewhere out in the sticks? At their call to worship, they ascend to the City of God, to the heavenly Jerusalem. They walk into the midst of innumerable angels (12:22). They come to general assembly of the universal Church and into the presence of God Himself (12:23). Scripture says this understanding should rattle us—we should start working out our salvation together with fear and trembling (Phil. 2:12–13). When we understand what is actually happening in a worship service, our contemporary flippancy evaporates. Since we are receiving a kingdom that cannot be shaken, we are to have grace so that *we* can serve (worship, *latreuo*) with reverence and godly fear (Heb. 12:28).

This godly fear should lead us to inquire how God wants us to approach Him. What are the elements of our worship service as we renew our covenant with God weekly? But first a word about this word *renewal,* which might be misunderstood. We do not renew our covenant with God because it was going to expire or run out, like a lease. We renew our covenant with God *because it is our life;* we renew covenant with God in worship the way food renews physical life or sexual communion renews marriage.

In the Old Testament, the sacrifices assigned by God had a particular order and placement—for an important reason. There were three offerings that were commonly found together, and when they were found together, they always followed a particular order (Lev. 9; 2 Chron. 29:20–36). First was the guilt offering (Lev. 17). Following this was the ascension offering, often misleadingly translated as burnt offering (Lev. 16:24–25). And third was the peace offering (Deut. 12:17–19). The guilt offering made the worshipper fit to enter into the presence of God. In the second offering, the worshipper ascended to God in the smoke of an offering that was entirely consumed on the altar. And the peace offering was a tangible demonstration that God had received the worshipper, and was willing to share fellowship with him in common meal.

We know of course that in the New Testament, the sacrifices of animals are done away with in the once-for-all sacrifice of Christ on the cross (Heb. 9:12). But the language of these Old Testament sacrifices does *not* disappear. Rather, sacrificial patterns under gird all new covenant worship. This is why we can understand the Bible as giving us a pattern of approach. First in the service, we confess our sins, which corresponds to the guilt offering. Then we offer ourselves up to God, without reserve or reluctance, which corresponds to the ascension offering. And then we sit down with God in the Lord's Supper, which corresponds to the peace offering. The heart of the service is bookended, at the beginning by the call to worship and at the conclusion by the benediction, a commissioning that sends the people of God out into the world to serve Him there (Rom. 12:1–2).

There are various legitimate ways in which this can be expressed, but in our church we have sought to structure our covenant renewal service in this way.[2] First is the *call* to worship,

---

[2] Jeffrey Meyers, *The Lord's Service* (Moscow: Canon Press, 2003).

which includes a prayer of adoration and a congregational singing of *Gloria in Excelsis.* Then is the element of *confession,* which includes an exhortation and a prayer of confession, assurance of pardon, and congregational singing of thanks. Next is the time of *consecration.* This includes the public reading of Scripture, the congregational time of prayer (petitions and thanks), the sermon, and a hymn or psalm of thanks. This time concludes with the offering brought forward in worship.[3] Then is the time of *communion,* where the Lord's Supper is observed. Last is the *commissioning,* where the people sing the *Gloria Patri* with hands upraised, receive a final charge, and the benediction. We have found God's promise true, as always. "I am the Lord thy God, which brought thee out of the land of Egypt: open thy mouth wide, and I will fill it" (Ps. 81:10).

All of this is glorious—why would anyone ever want to do anything else? "I was glad when they said unto me, let us go into the house of the Lord" (Ps. 122:1). The answer is that we live in a fallen world. It is far easier to let the garden fill up with weeds than to cultivate and tend it. A basic principle laid down by God holds true in worship, just as it does everywhere else. A man "becometh poor that dealeth with a slack hand: but the hand of the diligent maketh rich" (Prov. 10:4). Our contemporary worship is threadbare because we are lazy, and do not want to take the effort to study what God says about how we are to approach Him. Among other things, we are to approach Him *diligently.* He is "a rewarder of them that diligently seek him" (Heb. 11:6).

The reformation of the Church requires liturgical reformation, and our need is desperate. But when "the Lord shall build up Zion, he shall appear in his glory" (Ps. 102:16). We do not have fewer privileges than our brothers in the Old Testament did. Our place of worship is still "beautiful for situation,

---

[3] We do not pass the plate during worship—the money is collected in a box at the back, but it is brought forward as an act of worship.

the joy of the whole earth" (Ps. 48:2). But this is only true if we understand the character of God when we worship. We think of His lovingkindness, but we do it in the midst of His temple (Ps. 48:9).[4]

[4] A modified form of the section above appears in *Christ and His Rivals* (Athanasius Press, 2008).

— 6

THUNDERING THE WORD

B ut we are not to go through all these motions as though they were some kind of Indian rain dance, expecting the motions in themselves to haul down the blessings of God. The Word is always to accompany the sacrament; the Word is always to inform the people what they are doing and why; the Word is living and active, more powerful than any two-edged sword (Heb. 4:12–13). Without the Word, sacraments do not exist.

As worshippers, we are laid bare before this Word, and the Greek word describing this (*trachelizo*) is a word that refers to exposing the neck of a sacrificial animal just before the throat is cut. It is the Word that slays us, cuts us apart, assembles us on the altar, and sends us up to God in the smoke. Consequently, preachers need to learn to preach as though this is what is happening. First, we must handle the Word like a sword. And secondly, we must learn to handle the Word as though it were alive and has a mind of its own—because it does.

The apostle John brought Hellenistic philosophy crashing to earth when he taught us that the Word was in the beginning with God, that the Word was God, and that the Word then took on flesh and spent some time in Judea. The idea of an incarnate Logos was not really conducive to the Greek turn of mind. For them, the Logos was disembodied, abstract, unearthly—*spiritual*. But John said what he said, and Hellenistic civilization fell apart.

Christians therefore are people of words because they are people of the Word. But taken in isolation, without discussion, this is too facile. John did not say, "In the beginning was the frozen Noun." Parmenides was out. Neither did he exalt the tumultuous Verb because Heraclitus was equally rejected. *All* that words do must be carried by the Word, sustained by it. Words can have no real meaning apart from Him, and the Word cannot be outdone by His little imitators. When we observe the metaphorical potency of our words, this should not be thought of as a little moonlighting on the side. They have metaphorical potency only because of the Logos.

Gordon Clark goes too far when he equates the Logos with logic, but he does see that the Word must encompass all that words can do—his mistake was in underestimating what words were created by God to do.[5] Of course, words convey rational order, but they are by no means limited to this. Considering our familiar trinity of truth, goodness and beauty, we see that words do far more than simply communicate the *first* member of it. Words bring us the truth of the gospel, the goodness of the law, and the beauty of holiness—along with all the complex interrelationships between them. This being the case, the words of the sermons should exhibit this, and set an example for the saints of God.

Now one of the central duties of righteous words, including the righteous words of the preached Word, is the duty of conveying truth, goodness, and beauty through metaphor. And this means that we should look for the archetype of metaphors

[5] Gordon Clark, *Logic* (Jefferson: Trinity Foundation, 1985), xi.

in the Logos. Just as the Logos bears all true reason, so He embodies all true metaphor.

And we must watch our step here. We have been well-conditioned by modernism and post-modernism to miss the glory of metaphor. Although they pretend to be desperate enemies, they are actually running a good cop/bad cop drill on us. Both systems agree that metaphor is ultimately meaningless. Modernism says metaphor is meaningless and goes off to look for meaning in mathematical formulae, technological achievement, and other stainless steel accomplishments. Post-modernism says that metaphor is meaningless, and that everything is metaphor. Hence, everything is meaningless.

This is why right-minded Christians, whenever they hear some modern evangelical academic bemoaning the Enlightenment, have a spirit within them that pulls at the sleeve and says *uh oh*. They see, rightly, that the bemoaner is likely just another modernist, fleeing from the baying hounds of meaningless metaphors, and is now up a tree like a frightened raccoon, with the base of the tree surrounded by all the various forms of meaninglessness, each of them sitting patiently on his haunches. After a while, the academic despairs of rescue from the Enlightenment, climbs down the tree and becomes respectable in the current academy, which is to say, epistemological dogmeat.

There is an alternative: the acknowledgement that metaphor, far from keeping us away from meaning, is one of God's principal methods of bringing meaning to us. Metaphor, like an honest answer, is a kiss on the lips. How can we say this? The Logos is identified with God, and He is also distinguished from God. In the beginning was the Word and the Word was with God, and the Word was God. Is there a barrier of meaning between the Father and the Son? None at all. Jesus said that if someone had seen Him he had seen the Father. Jesus was the Way to the Father. According to Paul, Jesus is the visible image of the invisible Father and He is the exact representation of the divine Being. Put simply, Jesus Christ is like the Father, which means *He is ultimate metaphor.* He is not the Father, but as a distinct Person He nonetheless reveals the Father. He also is God, which means there can be no epistemological barrier between the Speaker and the Word.

God the Father speaks the Word, and the Word in His turn "speaks" about the Father through being spoken. In a similar way, my words reveal something about me, and so more is happening than my mind speaking words. My words also speak my mind. Within the Godhead, we see this operative truth. Metaphor plays an essential role in ultimate meaning.

Now this has direct implications for preaching and teaching. Those who are ministers of the Word must never consent to handle that Word in a truncated or wooden fashion. Such conservative and safe preaching is neither conservative nor safe. A preacher must never behave as though he were an engineer trying to write a phone book. God speaks the eternal Word of God, our Lord Jesus. He created the universe through Him. The universe is God speaking, and this is how the universe declares His glory—the heavens and earth speak through being spoken. The pulpit should be one of the liveliest places on earth, because in it, words are imitating the Word. This should never be done for the sake of mere entertainment; it is to be done in obedience.

Because of our sinfulness, God gave us the protection of His inscripturated Word, so that we might not be misled by our own lusts. But in the divine Word, with the example in Scripture of the Word enfleshed, the speech of our surrounding universe becomes intelligible. And so, guided by Scripture, we now know the meaning of rivers, mountains, deaths, burials, birds in flight, hot food, and cold water. And this is how we must texture our teaching and preaching. A word fitly spoken, an apt metaphor, will do more teaching, more revealing, than the most precisionistic word-chopping, lengthwise or otherwise. After all, the kingdom of God is like a pile of dead fish (Mt. 13:47).

So when a minister of Christ enters into the pulpit, he does so in order to declare and proclaim the Word of God. In order to do this, he must first handle the Word of God. And how shall he handle it? How shall he take this language of God, still hot from the ovens of heaven, and handle it without burning his fingers?

Of course we want to say that he should handle it wisely and well, but this is not helpful when it comes to the basics of exegesis. Wisely and well-handled *by what standard?* Most conservative evangelical pastors have been trained in what is called the historical/grammatical method of exegesis, but which might more accurately be called the *tight* historical/grammatical method. "Tight" means that the exegesis is limited to lexical study, syntactical study, and historical and contextual study, which is to say, Enlightenment exegesis. There is a difference between the responsible hermeneutic advocated by the Reformers (in contrast to allegorical and impudent excesses) and the "responsible" hermeneutic urged upon us today in the name of Science. The Reformers were sons of the Church, medieval men who saw that allegorical system of interpretation had gotten out of hand and needed to be reeled in. This is quite different from modern interpreters, sons of the Enlightenment, who heap abuse on edifying typology but then have a problem with scriptural counter-examples.

The New Testament creates a dilemma for the tight exegesis of scientism. As conservative ministers of the Word, we are fond of affirming the sufficiency of the Word for all things, and in all things. We do not need supplementary help from secular psychiatry, secular astrophysics, or any other branch of secular whatever in order to supplement the Scriptures. The problem is that we abandon this admirable stance when it comes to our method of getting at the Word of God.

Scripture is sufficient for all things, *including the task of teaching us how to learn from Scripture.* And does this not mean we should learn how to handle the Scriptures from the Lord Jesus and the apostles? The New Testament is filled with citations from the Old Testament, and we have more than enough material to show us how they handle the text. But this presents us with a problem of loyalties.

For example, moderns want to say that the "allegorical method" of interpretation arose because Greek philosophers were embarrassed by the shenanigans of their Homeric gods (whose authority could not be directly challenged), and so they devised allegorical interpretations to provide an edifying meaning for all Zeus' bedhopping. And this is true—that is exactly what happened. And so, they continue, the early church father Origen brought this fanciful exegesis into the church because he was swayed by such pagan allegorists (and by the Hellenistic Jewish allegorist Philo). As a result, the medieval church was brought under the pernicious influence of "edifying" allegorism.

Before replying to this historical reconstruction, let it first be said that allegoristic exegesis in the church *has* frequently been taken to excessive lengths, and has amounted to little more than an imbecilic trifling with the text. My personal favorite is the view that the Shulammite's belly, that lovely heap of wheat, actually represented the Great Sanhedrin. I picture a group of bearded rabbis sitting in a solemn assembly, and it just plain tickles me. Not my idea of a turn-on.

But such an historical sketch is simplistic. If the appeal to a *sensus plenior,* the fuller sense, came from Origen, or from other Alexandrians before him, then what are we to make of the very common assumption throughout the New Testament that the Old Testament had a *sensus plenior?* Where did Jesus and Paul get this hermeneutical technique? Did they get it from embarrassed Greek philosophers too? I am afraid we have honestly trained ourselves to miss what the New Testament writers are doing with the text, and we act like the early fathers received no encouragement whatsoever from the New Testament.

Christ was a Rock that followed the Jews in the wilderness (1 Cor. 10:3–4). The flood in Noah's time was a typological representation of Christian baptism. The bronze serpent in the wilderness was a type of the crucifixion. Sarah and Hagar were representative types of two covenants. Melchizedek was a type of Christ, and the etymological history of his city—Salem, meaning peace—was also typologically significant. The writers of the New Testament certainly saw Christ in the Old when He was expressly predicted ("A virgin will conceive"), but it has to be said that they also saw Him *everywhere else.* And Jesus showed the way; our Lord Jesus was the one who taught them this hermeneutic. "And beginning at Moses and all the prophets, he expounded unto them in all the Scriptures the things concerning himself" (Lk. 24:27).

So then the question becomes whether we the uninspired are to imitate their handling of the Scripture, or whether this is a "don't-try-this-at-home" kind of thing. If the latter, then how and where does Scripture teach us our hermeneutic, the one we *are* supposed to use at home? If the former, then we have to learn how uninspired men can learn from inspired men how to handle the Scriptures. In his book on this subject, Richard Longenecker allows that various forms of typological exegesis are very common in the New Testament but wants to say that we should not attempt this apart from special revelation. For him, literal exegesis is safe—staying close to the shore.[6]

The problem here is that when Jesus (to take one example) teaches His two disciples on the road to Emmaus about these things, He rebukes them for not having read the Old Testament in this way already—and this was apart from special revelation. In other words, we do not abstain from this method

[6] Richard Longenecker, *Biblical Exegesis in the Apostolic Period* (Grand Rapids: Eerdmans, 1975), 185–198.

of exegesis (rightly performed) because we are concerned for exegetical prudence, but rather because we are slow of heart to believe everything the prophets have spoken.

Of course the question immediately arises—where are the brakes on this thing? Why is the "erotic rabbis" interpretation wrong? Of course, the concern is in principle correct. Given the sin and folly still resident in any interpreter, we always need to know where the brakes are. The full answer is that Christ is Lord. And, as an afterthought, we need to remember that every hermeneutic needs brakes, and not just the typological school. And the Enlightenment hermeneutic is a three-hundred-and-fifty-year-old runaway train.

But we still have to answer the question. Where are the brakes on *this* system of interpretation? How can we handle Scripture in this way without flying off into fanciful or frivolous interpretations? The fact that other schools of interpretation have to answer the same question does not mean that *we* have answered it.

So, how should we begin our lessons in a sober and biblically grounded typology? Perhaps an analogy can help. Consider the text of the New Testament on a single sheet as an overlay for the Old. The Old Testament is a single sheet underneath. Every place the New Testament interprets the Old in a particular way, (metaphorically) drive a nail through both testaments. Have the New Testament *set* the meaning of every Old Testament passage it addresses.

What does this do to the passages that are not addressed directly? The passages that we *have* fixed in place limit our range of motion. To illustrate, to understand Adam as a type of Christ is settled by the New Testament (Rom. 5; 1 Cor. 15). Adam had a wife named Eve (Gen. 3:20), and Christ has a bride also—the Church (Eph. 5:25). If we were to call the Church the last Eve, we are saying something that Scripture does not explicitly say anywhere, but which Scripture does implicitly require. Our fixed points of reference require this of us.

We cannot consistently deny that the Church is an Eve—she is married to an Adam.

But if we were to say that Eve is a type of "Madaleine Albright listening to the United Nations serpent" and that the Second Coming was therefore three weeks away, then we are exercising our imaginations, not interpreting Scripture. Our interpretation amounts to little more than that common vocabulary exercise in elementary schools, where the students are told to write a story using this week's vocabulary words. Very few objective constraints are put on such works of imagination. The Madaleine Albright illustration is biblical interpretation only because biblical vocabulary words, like Eve, are used in it. As C.S. Lewis once said of fanciful interpretation, if the text had had small pox, the sermon wouldn't have caught it.

An exercise that could be very helpful to pastors in accomplishing this mindset is one that was instrumental in helping me shake loose of many of the unbiblical doctrinal assumptions I had picked up over the years. Most copies of the New Testament mark citations from the Old in some way. The unfortunate thing is that the reverse is not usually done—those places in the Old Testament which are quoted later on in the New are rarely marked as such. The thing to do is to fix the problem yourself with marker pens. Look up every place in the Old Testament which is quoted in the New and mark it with a highlighter. Then off in the margin write down the New Testament reference where it is quoted.

When this is done, read through the Old Testament, and you will be continually reminded that the New Testament contains authoritative teaching on the marked Old Testament passages. For example, when you come to Psalm 2, you are reminded at once that there is teaching on *what this psalm means* in multiple places in the New Testament.

The first thing that will become apparent is that Jesus and His apostles had favorite books and passages. Anyone who wants to grasp the teaching of the New Testament has to master Genesis, Deuteronomy, Psalms, and Isaiah, which are quoted in the New Testament constantly. And the way to learn these Old Testament books (and all the others) is to learn what the New Testament says about them. But this is rarely done. Any preacher who uses commentaries when preaching through Old Testament books can testify how rare it is for the apostolic interpretation to be taken into any kind of account by the commentator as he seeks to find the *meaning* of the text before him. Surely this should be a cause of astonishment. Sometimes commentators do have to deal with the troubles *caused* by an apostle—as in, "How can we reconcile him saying this with our knowledge that he was both inspired and not to be listened to? But I have yet to find a commentator on Genesis, for example, who says that Genesis 6 is clearly a passage where we learn the nature and meaning of Christian baptism, and then goes on to exposit this truth. And furthermore, I am not holding my breath.

The modernist approach to the text is to interpret it according to certain modernist rules, and to the extent the apostolic teaching is referenced at all, it provides anachronistic embarrassment. Once, while taking a class on hermeneutics at an evangelical seminary, I heard the instructor say that Paul was, and I quote, "wrong" in his handling of Hagar and Sarah. But this instructor never would have dreamed of saying that the academic experts were wrong about Genesis because they didn't see two covenants in these women.

Some might still be suspicious of reasoning "by good and *literary* consequence" from fixed reference points. In the abstract, it can sound scary, but it is still academic. Most of us could spend several profitable years discovering how thoroughly typological the New Testament handling of the Old Testament actually is in all the "fixed" places. Even if we never take a step beyond that, we will still find ourselves with a much richer understanding of the Word than we currently have. And if we do take the next step, as we should, we will simply be following dominical and apostolic leadership.

If all this still smells too much of the study, consider an example of how this approach would translate to the pulpit—and how edifying it would be to the people of God.

In the greatest calamity that ever befell our race, our father Adam abdicated his assigned role as the guardian of his wife and family. This took place when Adam was standing in the shade of a particular tree in a particular garden, and it was not that long ago. Our mother Eve was there too, and as she reached for the fruit, she did so in the grip of the lust of the eyes (1 Jn. 2:16; Gen. 3:6), the lust of the flesh (1 Jn. 2:16; Gen. 3:6), and the pride of life (1 Jn.; Gen. 3:6). She was deceived, and this is not surprising because she had not yet been brought out of Adam's side when God had given him the prohibition. Adam, however, knew of the restriction directly from God, and yet he stood by, mute. He was close enough to take the fruit from Eve's hand once she had eaten it (Gen. 3:6). He was *with* her. And this is why Scripture says that sin entered the world through one man, and not through one woman (Rom. 5:17).

In this calamity, at this fateful tree, we all rebelled against God. When Adam sinned, we sinned in him and through him (Rom. 5:12). God in His wisdom has created mankind (or, to use the Hebrew word for mankind, *Adam*) in such a way that we were all covenantally connected in one man. When it comes to sin, we are all close cousins. We *are* mankind. We *are* Adam. And we all sinned at the tree. God determined to provide us with a salvation that works in the same covenantal way that our loss of innocence did. Just as the disobedience of our father Adam (at a tree) plunged us into darkness, so the obedience of our father the second Adam (at another tree) resulted in our salvation.

But there are differences. In the first instance, God gave Eve to Adam, and then the disobedience followed. In our salvation, this order is reversed. God gave the second Adam a bitter cup to drink, and He drank it while hanging on a tree under the curse of God. And at that moment, a soldier on the ground took another piece of wood—the shaft of a spear—and became the instrumental cause of the creation of a bride for the second Adam. An Adam is not fully an Adam without an Eve, and this second Eve is the Christian church. And the second Eve came from the side of her Adam, just as the first Eve had done.

The first Adam was put into a deep sleep (amounting to a coma) in order for Eve to be taken from his side. This sleep is an obvious type of death. When the Lord Jesus died, He fulfilled this type—He had fallen into His deep "sleep." And at that moment, a spear was rammed into his side, and the apostle John takes great pains to explain how important this moment was. "But one of the soldiers with a spear pierced his side, and forthwith came there out blood and water. And he that saw it bare record, and his record is true: and he knoweth that he saith true, *that ye might believe*" (Jn. 19:34–35). Mark it well, John says—there was blood and water that came from the Lord's side. Why is this important? So that you might believe.

Blood and water came from His side, and the Spirit bore witness to this through John, and in that blood and water we find the formation of the Christian Church. "This is he that came by water and blood, even Jesus Christ; not by water only, but by water and blood" (1 Jn. 5:6). This water and blood is very important—it is the basis of our witness and identity. Christ came by water and blood, and this is why we come by water and blood. And this is also why we as believers must testify to it in this way. "And there are three that bear witness in earth, the Spirit, and the water, and the blood: and these three agree in one" (1 Jn. 5:8; cf. Jn. 3:5).

Jesus Christ is our second Adam—Scripture is explicit on this point. Christ is a bridegroom—there is no room for discussion on this point either. So who does an Adam marry?

She shall be called Eve, because she is mother of all the living (Gen. 3:20). Who is this woman, this new Eve? She, too, is the mother of us all—the glorious Christian Church.

> But Jerusalem which is above is free, *which is the mother of us all.* For it is written, Rejoice, thou barren that bearest not; break forth and cry, thou that travailest not: for the desolate hath many more children than she which hath an husband. (Gal. 4:26–27)

Individually, we believers are the sons and daughters of the second Adam and second Eve. The Church is our mother, and Christ is our Father (Is. 9:6). Corporately, gathered together in worship we are the bride of Christ, and He is our husband.

Unlike our first husband, unlike our first father, the Lord Jesus has not abdicated. He has not abandoned the priestly duty that was assigned to Him—the priestly duty of guarding and protecting His wife, and all the children God gave to Him. Collectively, we are that wife, and individually, we are those children. And this is why the Lord Jesus is able to say, "Behold I and the *children* which God hath given me" (Heb. 2:13).

As pastors, these are the things we must declare and preach if we are to recover an understanding our proper *identity* as the Church. Adam stood by when Eve was deceived because he had forgotten *where she came from.* The second Adam will never do this—but the second Eve periodically does. We forget where we came from. We forget our birthplace. We were created when the Lord Jesus died on a beam of wood, and another shaft of wood drove a spearhead into Him. That spearhead was the culmination of a grotesque judicial murder. But the folly of man is wisdom to God, and so when the spear went in, the Bride of the Lord came out. And at this second tree, the treachery of our race was undone forever.

— 7

BONE OF HIS BONES

An important part of all this is learning to see the importance of feeding at the Lord's Table regularly. One of the pronounced features of covenant renewal worship is the observance of *weekly* communion. In the Supper of the Lord, we are being built up into a perfect man—we are in the process of being knit together. This being the case, we should not want this knitting of the Spirit to be limited to a quarterly or monthly event.

And if we recall what we have already learned about how we tend to read the Scriptures as a private collection of inspirational quotes, we can perhaps start trying to see them in their corporate, sacramental significance. Because this is a subject on which historic prejudices run deep, it is important to be clear at the outset. Covenant renewal in the Lord's Supper is not a doctrine which in any way countenances the Roman Catholic error of seeing a transformation in the elements of bread and wine themselves. Nothing happens magically to the bread or in the wine, just as gold being slipped on a finger in a wedding ceremony has the same molecular make-up as gold anywhere else.

But equally rejected is the rationalistic superstition which maintains that in the Supper of the Lord nothing happens apart from our rolling certain sentences around in our heads. The Supper is far more than a mere memory aid. In this minimalist view, because we can roll those sentences around at any time, under any circumstances, the bread, and the wine, and the congregation, all become dispensable. But contrary to both these views, and in line with the historic Protestant view, in the Lord's Supper, something is really happening that cannot happen anywhere else, or by other means. God's grace is certainly not limited to the Supper, but in this communion of the saints, God has committed Himself to bestow a certain gracious blessing that is not bestowed elsewhere.

Several scriptural examples should suffice to establish this.

> I speak as to wise men; judge ye what I say. The cup of blessing which we bless, is it not the communion of the blood of Christ? The bread which we break, is it not the communion of the body of Christ? For we being many are one bread, and one body: for we are all partakers of that one bread. Behold Israel after the flesh: are not they which eat of the sacrifices partakers of the altar? What say I then? that the idol is any thing, or that which is offered in sacrifice to idols is any thing? But I say, that the things which the Gentiles sacrifice, they sacrifice to devils, and not to God: and I would not that ye should have fellowship with devils. Ye cannot drink the cup of the Lord, and the cup of devils: ye cannot be partakers of the Lord's table, and of the table of devils. Do we provoke the Lord to jealousy? are we stronger than he? (1 Cor. 10:15–22)

The cup of blessing was the third cup of the Passover meal. This cup, a cup of blessing, is the cup that Christians are privileged to drink to the end of the world. Now a blessing is a benediction. It is true *blessing*. Like all covenant blessings, when it is despised and insulted it becomes a fearsome curse, but nevertheless Paul calls it a cup of blessing. When we come in faith, it is blessing. When we come to it in any manner of unbelief, the Lord judges His people. At Corinth, many were sick and had died because of how they mishandled this blessing.

It is important for us to realize that the world is covenantal in its structure. Every one eats from one of two tables. Either we partake with Christ, or we partake with demons. This partaking is a covenantal reality in both cases. Old Testament priests partook of the altar. Pagan worshippers partake of their sacrifices. And we partake of Christ.

The reason it is a blessing is because it is the communion of the blood of Christ. The word communion here is *koinonia*—fellowship, partaking, communion. When someone in faith partakes of the wine he is partaking of the blood of Christ. Not, as was said before, because the wine has been transformed, but rather because *we are being transformed*. It is the same with the bread. We partake of one loaf because *we are the one loaf*. When Paul says later in his discussion that we must discern the Lord's body, he is not telling us that we must adore the elements on the table (the Roman Catholic error) or muck around inside our own hearts looking for hidden sin (the Protestant pietist error). We are to discern the Lord's body *in one another*. When the Lord's Supper is being served, we should sit up straight, and look around the congregation, eyes open, up and down our row. It is true that we are to examine ourselves, but we are to do so in relation to one another. We must not curl up into a little ball, close our eyes, and try to establish a private, spiritual moment with Jesus. We are one loaf, we are in this together, we are being built up into a perfect man.

> There is one body, and one Spirit, even as ye are called in one hope of your calling; One Lord, one faith, one baptism, One God and Father of all, who is above all, and through all, and in you all . . . And he gave some, apostles; and some, prophets; and some, evangelists; and some,

pastors and teachers; For the perfecting of the saints, for the work of the ministry, for the edifying of the body of Christ: Till we all come in the unity of the faith, and of the knowledge of the Son of God, unto a perfect man, unto the measure of the stature of the fulness of Christ . . . But speaking the truth in love, may grow up into him in all things, which is the head, even Christ: From whom the whole body fitly joined together and compacted by that which every joint supplieth, according to the effectual working in the measure of every part, maketh increase of the body unto the edifying of itself in love. (Eph. 4:4–16)

What is God doing? What is He up to? He is bringing us into the fullness of Christ. He is knitting the whole body together. He is working out the unity of the faith, the knowledge of the Son of God, until we all come to a perfect man. We need to see that this passage begins by telling us to maintain a unity that we already have. This unity is given to us on the basis of our unified faith—one Lord, one faith, one baptism. This is not the end of the process, but rather the beginning. Having brought us together, God then establishes a ministry in our midst in order that this ministry might be His instrument for accomplishing His greater goal of perfect unity. This ministry consists of apostles, prophets, evangelists, and pastor/teachers. And what, specifically, do the pastor/teachers do? They oversee the ministry of Word and sacrament. What does this ministry do? It causes the whole body to be fitly joined together. And faithful pastors do not have the authority to dispense with instruments thought by the apostles to be essential to this process. Simply put, we do not have the authority to turn sermons into lectures and sacraments into options.

Our goal should be to approach God corporately in worship, with the culmination of that worship being the peace offering, the Supper of the Lord, the partaking of the blood and body of Christ in true *koinonia*. We must not forget this element of partaking. "But to do good and to communicate (*koinonia*) forget not: for with such sacrifices God is well pleased" (Heb. 13:16). Do not forget to *communicate.* This does not refer to talking, and does not refer to the coffee and donuts in the fellowship hall after services (although that is a distant cousin of this). We partake together, of one another, around the Table of the Lord, in the bread and in the cup.

> Having therefore, brethren, boldness to enter into the holiest by the blood of Jesus, By a new and living way, which he hath consecrated for us, through the veil, that is to say, his flesh; And having an high priest over the house of God; Let us draw near with a true heart in full assurance of faith, having our hearts sprinkled from an evil conscience, and our bodies washed with pure water. Let us hold fast the profession of our faith without wavering; (for he is faithful that promised;) And let us consider one another to provoke unto love and to good works: Not forsaking the assembling of ourselves together, as the manner of some is; but exhorting one another: and so much the more, as ye see the day approaching. (Heb. 10:19–25)

Together, corporately, we have a high priest. We (notice, *we*) may draw near with a true heart in full assurance of faith. We can do this because our hearts were sprinkled and our bodies were washed. In other words, we have been baptized. But in order to have this confidence of faith, it is not just bodies washed, but hearts sprinkled. We hold fast to our profession, and we do it without wavering. We are not to forsake the gathering of ourselves together, as some do. We are to exhort one another, which is what this paragraph is doing. Come together. But what do we do when we come together? The answer is found at the beginning of this passage. We boldly assemble in order to enter into the holiest place *by the blood of Jesus.* We do this by a new and living way—which is described here as the veil, or, put another way, *His flesh.*

This is a living way. We do not partake of a dead Christ, but rather a resurrected and living Christ. We partake of Him *by means of faith,* which means that we do as we are told. We take and eat *by faith.* We take and drink *by faith.* As we do this, we are becoming what we eat. And since what we are eating is a new humanity, resurrected and alive, never to die again, we are becoming that new humanity, a perfect man. Do not look for transformations in the wrong bread. Look for transformations in the bread of the larger body, the Church.

If we were to say that since the operative word in all this is faith, and that this means that we can go out by ourselves, gin up some faith, and receive these blessings, we are showing that we do not understand the first thing about what faith does. Faith *obeys.* If God says "take and eat, and do so in faith," and we turn this into "do *not* take and do *not* eat, but still have faith," we are showing nothing but our impudence. God told us where we were to meet with Him, and we are to meet with Him there. The fact that others came to the Table in superstition, thus avoiding a sacramental union with Him, is not any basis for us to avoid that same sacramental union another way. One man ducks down an alley to avoid meeting with God on the street. Do we escape *his* error by choosing a different alley to duck down?

One last comment about covenant renewal and the Supper of the Lord. A pastor can fully expect and anticipate that moving to weekly communion will cause quite a bit of sin to be uncovered in the congregation. This is not a sign that things are falling apart, but rather the opposite. In the Supper, God is *dealing with us,* and in dealing with us, He always addresses our sins. If a congregation perseveres in this, the people will come to the point of deep gratitude. He is our God, and we are His people.

— 8

THE PSALMS
AS BATTERING RAM

The music of the Church has been steadily deteriorating for generations. The lyrics have been consistently dumbed down, and the music has gotten progressively more simplistic. We are now at the point where, in our corporate laziness, we have trite worship choruses that have almost no biblical or doctrinal content, and what little content there is gets sung over and over again in a mantra-like fashion.

Like many such things, this is a reaction and rebellion against a degraded but higher form. In other words, doing the easier thing is always . . . easier. One form of laziness is to do the more demanding thing badly, and this breeds a reaction which insists on doing an easier thing. And so when those who are committed to doing the more difficult thing behave in such a way as to incite a revolt, everyone takes advantage of the opportunity, and with enthusiasm. One of my favorite hymns today is *Holy, Holy, Holy*, but when I was a boy I *hated* that song. In the church where I grew up, the hymn was sung like a dirge at God's funeral. When I first encountered contemporary worship music, it was a like a spring day after a long winter. But simple reaction and relief do not constitute a biblical approach to worship music.

The Bible teaches us that our faith is to be robust, and our zeal apparent. This should come out in everything we do, but particularly in how we sing. We are told that we are to let the word of Christ dwell in us richly, and that the overflow of this is to be the singing of psalms, hymns and spiritual songs (Col. 3:16). Now the overflow of something rich will be itself rich. If our faith in Christ is rich, if His Word is dwelling in us richly, then the lyrics of our psalms should be rich, the melodies rich, the harmonization rich, and the robust and joyful singing of them should be rich. Our public worship of God should be like every other aspect of our Christian lives—we should be "fervent in spirit; serving the Lord" (Rom. 12:11).

When difficult and demanding music is performed in the Church, over time it tends to fall into one of two traps. First, it can become nothing more than a matter of professionalism. Musicianship is first, and the quality of the musicians' lives becomes less important. After some time, it is not even necessary that the performers (since it is now a *performance*) even be Christian. Under this scenario, the talent is there, but the integrity, passion, and glory of worship has departed. Another common trap is for the more demanding music to become simple traditionalism. In other words, the older and more rigorous hymns are still sung, but a definite lethargy sets in. The people know the music, and are comfortably bored with it. They have no intention of changing anything—they worship God this way because it is easy to do so. In this scenario, the material is there, but the integrity, passion, and glory of worship has departed by another route.

In the midst of such spiritual lethargy, it is not surprising that many have been attracted to contemporary worship music. At least (and at the beginning this is a true strength), there is *life* involved with it, and it is also understandable. After all, Paul says that he would rather sing with his mind in small quantities than unintelligibly in much greater quantities.

> What is it then? I will pray with the spirit, and I will pray with the understanding also: I will sing with the spirit, and I will sing with the understanding also. Else when thou shalt bless with the spirit, how shall he that occupieth the room of the unlearned say Amen at thy giving of thanks, seeing he understandeth not what thou sayest? For thou verily givest thanks well, but the other is not edified. I thank my God, I speak with tongues more than ye all: Yet in the church I had rather speak five words with my understanding, that by my voice I might teach others also, than ten thousand words in an unknown tongue. (1 Cor. 14:15–19)

And this is what has happened to us. Many Christians have made this kind of choice. They much prefer the accessibility of contemporary forms of worship to the inaccessible worship they remember from when they were kids. But *why* was the more traditional forms of music inaccessible to them? I would suggest that it was inaccessible because of the attitude that had developed toward it—mere professionalism or bored traditionalism—and not because of the music itself. And a man who is impatient with something does not need much encouragement to be enticed with an alternative.

So we must beware of the false dilemma. It *would* be far better to sing five intelligible words (accompanied with three chords) than ten thousand unintelligible Latin or German words borne along by glorious cantatas. It *would* be better to sing a Scripture chorus to a humming guitar than to sing an old psalm in common meter in such a way that the psalm-singing was hard to distinguish from the snoring. But this is not the only choice we have. What is better, to sing five glorious words or five hundred glorious words? What is better, three good chords, or seventeen rich chords? It is assumed in covenant renewal worship that we want to sing with fervency, and with content, zeal, and biblical consistency. This means a return to the psalms.

As we encourage this return to the psalms, a few things should be noted. The attitude should be one of gladness and joy. "Is anyone merry?" James asked. Then let him sing psalms (Jas. 5:13). The heart should be ready for discipline. We are in the process of recovering a musical heritage that we have been throwing away for several centuries now, so we will not recover it in ten minutes. We will not have a convenience store reformation. And last, the attitude that returns to the psalms properly is one that understands what a privilege this is. We do not do this because we have to sing psalms. We do it because God *lets* us.

When the recovery of psalms is well underway, a few interesting discoveries emerge. First, a person may have been a Christian for fifty years, but he will find himself singing things he has never sung (or said) before. These things are all in God's songbook, and so we should ask ourselves why we have not been singing the *kind* of thing that God assigned us to sing. There are many aspects of this, but I will conclude this section by noting just one of them. The psalmist had enemies, and he dealt with them in the music. The psalter is a battle hymnal. If we are serious about conquering the world with the gospel through biblical worship, we will soon discover that it cannot be done without the psalms. What is a good thing to sing while swinging a battering ram at the gates of the enemy? There are many to choose from, but why not Psalm 68? "God shall arise and by His might, put all His enemies to flight."

— 9

FEASTING AND THE SABBATH

Those who love the fourth commandment do not need to be reminded how much God's Word is openly disregarded at this point. Business as usual down at the mall is the order of the day, and the frantic 24-7 pace of American life shows no sign of slowing down. There is no rest, as it was said, for the wicked (Is. 57:21).

But within the Reformed world, we need to concern ourselves with sabbath-breaking by the ostensible *friends* of the fourth commandment. This is particularly the case for those churches just coming to settled convictions on the sabbath. Overreaction is a very real temptation. The nature and limits of our sabbath convictions are very important, because there is more than one way to break a commandment.

When Jesus had His famous collisions with the Pharisees over sabbath-keeping, He was not dealing with people who openly rejected the legitimacy of the commandment. He was in a conflict with those who would be *called* sabbatarians. In these various gospel narratives, more is taught to us than the fact that Jesus was exonerated from the false charge of sabbath-breaking. The wisdom of His responses showed that His opponents, filled with scruples about the fourth commandment, were the *real* sabbath breakers. Not only was Christ exonerated on the charge, His adversaries were convicted by the very charge they leveled against Him.

So we see that the sabbath can be broken, not only by those who walk away from it in contempt, but also by those who swing it around in such a way as to bloody the noses of others. The problem of sabbatarian sabbath-breaking can begin very subtly. It has taken hold when the first question asked is, "What am I *not* allowed to do on Sunday?" The desire for such direction is a very natural one, but if we are not careful, the end result will be a rabbinical ruling on whether it is lawful to shoot hoop in the driveway, or push buttons on the microwave. Of course, we will at some point choose to avoid certain things on the Lord's Day, but we must ensure that it is the natural result of what we have embraced—the sabbath is a *positive* ordinance.

Within our reformational ranks, a common understanding of the Lord's Day follows the Westminster Confession when it says that the sabbath should be filled up with three kinds of work—works of necessity, works of piety, and works of mercy. As the Confession puts it, in righteous sabbath-keeping, men "are taken up *the whole time* in the publick and private exercises of his worship, and in the duties of necessity and mercy" (XXI/viii, emphasis mine). But something is missing here—rest—and rest is the centerpiece of the commandment as it is found in Scripture. The Bible does not say that we are to work for six days, and then on the seventh day, we are to, well, work at these other three jobs. Rather, we are commanded to *rest*.

Perhaps a better statement of our obligation with regard to the commandment would be this: on the first day of the week, we are commanded to rest before the Lord (Exod. 20:8). In addition, we are commanded to interrupt this rest with time set aside for corporate worship (Lev. 23:1–3). This worship is celebratory, and so for most of the participants it is another form of rest. Those, like ministers, who have to work during this time are nonetheless guiltless, because the work is required of them by God (Mt. 12:5). Throughout the rest of the day, works of necessity are of course permitted (Mk. 2:27), as well as works of mercy and kindness (Mk. 3:4). These latter two works are *permitted,* not required.

Another problem can develop as well. Among many sabbatarians, a minimalist and negative approach to the commandment has taken root. To take a swing at one of our favorite whipping boys, this amounts to *gnostic* sabbatarianism. "Spiritual" observance minimalizes physical activity, as though work were defined by a high school physics textbook—expenditure of energy. But this would exclude preparation of a nice meal, lovemaking, or walking in the park. Bit by bit, the ideal sabbath becomes a day of staring at dull wallpaper, sipping tepid water and nibbling on a cracker.

But the passage in Leviticus shows us that the weekly sabbath was one of their holy festivals. It was a *feast.* The early Christians carried this same idea over, feasting together on the Lord's Day. Paul urged feasting on the Lord's Day. "Therefore let us keep the feast, not with old leaven, neither with the leaven of malice and wickedness; but with the unleavened bread of sincerity and truth" (1 Cor. 5:8). This exhortation was necessary in Corinth because their sabbath feasting had apparently gotten out of hand (1 Cor. 11:20–22). Jude wrote to some Christians who had to deal with false teachers intruding upon the holy festival (Jude 12).

So the church should of course urge and teach faithful sabbath keeping. But it should be done positively. First, leave room for rest. The programs of the church should not fill every little nook and cranny of the day. And the worship should be the kind of worship the saints look forward to all week. For the remainder of the day, the teaching should emphasize that this is a day for joy, gladness, hot food, good wine, fellowship with friends, singing psalms, reading books, and reciting poetry. In the time left over, arrange the couch so it is near a window in the middle of your loveliest sun puddle. And take a nap.

10

WORSHIP HAS A FUTURE

One of the great problems of the modern Reformed world is the tendency to look at the covenant through the lens of election instead of looking at election through the lens of the covenant. This is not said in an attempt to back away from the doctrine of election at all. The Bible teaches it, and so should we, and there are of course settings when the Scriptures tell us to use that "lens" of election to see more clearly. During a time of persecution, the doctrine of election can be an enormous comfort. Who will lay a charge against God's elect? It is *God* who justifies (Rom. 8).

But as a general pattern, Scripture places the words of the covenant in our mouths, and these are the words we are to speak in our households and to our children—we are to live inductively from the terms of the covenant, not deductively from the abstract truth of election. This should be obvious. We do not know the names of the elect. But we *do* know the names of the covenant members all around us. We are told to make our calling and election sure, which is what we do through faith as we continue in covenant faithfulness. We are not told to make our place in the covenant sure through continuation in trying to divine the names on the roster of the elect. The secret things belong to God (Deut. 29:29), but the things revealed belong to us *and to our children.* The details of election reside with God. The stipulations of the covenant are in the Bible right there in our lap.

All of this has important ramifications for our children. When we start with the doctrine of election as a theological datum, and reason from there, apportioning the blessings as we go, by the time we come to our children, there often is nothing left for them. Because we cannot see election, we have devised another indicator of election which we cannot see either, but it is easier for us to *pretend* that we can see it. We pretend to be able to see whether or not a heart is genuinely converted.

Whenever these two things are found together—strong Calvinism and pietistic conversionism—children are regularly mangled by the covenant people of God instead of nurtured by them. Jesus pronounced a solemn warning against anyone who stumbled the little ones, and this is a warning that ought to be heeded in our circles far more thoughtfully and submissively than it is.

So in setting forth what is sometimes called the doctrine of covenantal succession, I do not want to emphasize the proofs. This is because we must be repenting of our idolatrous rationalism. Consequently, I want to start by describing, with scriptural terminology, what it is like to believe and live this way. In this way, perhaps those who are opposed to this teaching, or those who have concerns about it, may at least see what it feels like before the controversy starts. And perhaps they might muse for a moment on how wonderful this would be if it *were* true. Having done this, we can turn to what results are produced by unbelief in these promises, and lastly, we can consider the promises themselves.

The key to understanding this aspect of the covenant is not primarily argumentation, but rather *faith.* Everything must to be done in the context of faith. *Credo ut intelligam*—"I believe

in order that I may understand." It is not until we believe God
for our children that we can begin to understand our children,
or the promises concerning them. How could it be otherwise?

In countless places, God promises Himself to us and to
our children. He never gives Himself outside the boundaries of
a covenant, and this gift is no exception. He will be our God,
and we will be His people. In giving this gift to us, He does not
do it with the understanding that the human partakers of the
covenant are somehow perfect. When God keeps covenant over
many generations, as He promises to do in many places, He
promises as part of this to *show mercy* to those who love Him,
and have faith in Him. This showing of mercy shows that the
key which unlocks the covenant is not perfection, but faith.
Or, rather, it is not our *own* perfection. Christ kept the terms of
the covenant perfectly, and when we believe God in the name
of Jesus Christ, His perfect obedience is imputed to us. The
instrument which God uses to bring this blessing to us is faith.
And, just in case we are tempted to put on airs because we were
shrewd enough to have faith, Paul dryly informs us that even
that faith is a gift.

The initial blessing of the covenant which is appropriated
by faith is that of justification. But it was never intended to
stop there. Our life in the covenant is from faith to faith. In
numerous places we are told that the just shall *live* by faith. The
prophet does not say that the just shall commence by faith, and
then finish through sheer dint of human strivings. Everything
we do, everything we say, is to be set apart and sanctified by
faith. This is not controversial, but let us move it on over into
controversial territory.

The covenant blessings of God include many blessings
which are less than salvation itself. All of them are appropriated
by faith, working through love, faith that is true faith, from
beginning to end. God promises to answer prayer, for example.
Does this mean that if a believer disbelieves in a particular
matter of prayer that he has lost his salvation? Of course not,

but he certainly (at the least) has lost the blessing of answered prayer.

God promises us the salvation of our children. We see in Scripture, and in the Christian world around us, many examples where the children of the covenant are not saved. Does this mean the Word of God is of no effect? Of course not—*let God be true and every man a liar.* If God has promised us our children as part of the covenant, our duty is to look at the Word of God in faith, and repent of casting sidelong glances at other people's children.

It is a fact that many covenant children fall away. Apostasy is a real sin, committed by real people. But this does not set aside the promises. Do we really want to say that those who stagger in their faith while at prayer have the authority to nullify all the promises made concerning prayer? And if not, then why do we want to reason the same way concerning our children? So every child we beget, conceive, bear, carry, spank, feed, rock, teach, comfort, discipline, and love is to grow up in an atmosphere of faith. This faith is a faith in the God who always keeps covenant and mercy to a thousand generations.

What happens when we do not live before God in this faith? We continue to teach our children inescapably, somehow, some way. I do not want to overstate this, or state it in a way that brings unnecessary grief to parents. But the reason we must proceed anyway is that something has to be done about all the *children* who are being brought to grief the way we do things now. I have seen many Reformed believers literally chase their children away from salvation. We have somehow come to think the bread of life is a choking hazard.

We all know the problem of overt hypocrisy—where a father is saintly at church but tyrannical and obnoxious at home. When children in such a home flee from the Christian faith, the reasons are obvious. But the problem we have in Reformed circles is far more insidious than this. Of course we all have to struggle with the impact of our sins on our children.

But the problem we are discussing here is the impact of our "virtues" on the children. We are talking about believers who take the good stout rope of their pietistic traditions, and tie their children up lest they get under the table to gather crumbs with the son of the Syro-Phoenecian woman.

A young child comes to his father and says that he wants to believe in Jesus. The father, trained in the tenets of pietism, does not believe that this could possibly be sincere or genuine. In a Baptist home, the child is kept away from baptism, and in a Presbyterian home, he is kept away from the Lord's Table. But he is young and pliable. He knows that he does not know a lot—he trusts his father on this, and more's the pity. The father says in effect, by keeping him at arm's length from any covenant blessings, that his profession of faith and trust is more worthy of doubt than credence, and this is the first (twisted) covenantal lesson the child learns. Christian parents are commanded to teach their children to believe, and instead, in the name of high conversion standards, *we teach them to doubt.* Then, when they grow up and mature in the doubting that *we* have taught them, we point to that doubt as clear evidence that we did the right thing in keeping them away in the first place.

It is as though we withhold food from our children because they are not yet big and strong. Grow up to be big and strong, and *then* we can give you some food. But they don't grow (not having any food), and then, when they finally die of starvation, we shake our heads sadly. Such is the grip of our revivalist theology that we actually do not notice what we are doing to them. The (covenantal) death of the child is then, in all seriousness, treated, after the fact, as a good reason for not having fed him.

This is not what we find in the Bible. The children of God's servants will *continue,* and their descendants will be *established* before the Lord God (Ps. 102:28). God is a jealous God, visiting the consequences of idolatry to the third and fourth generation— but to those who love Him, the blessings flow for *thousands* of generations (Deut. 5:9–10; 7:9). God keeps covenant and mercy with our great, great great grandchildren. He thinks more of them than we do. But nevertheless, we, the children of Abraham, will inherit the world through the righteousness of faith, and not through works of the law (Rom. 4:13). The God who makes sons of Abraham out of rocks can certainly make sons of Abraham out of sons of Abraham (Mt. 3:9). David, the servant of God, is now king over us, and he will be our prince forever, in an everlasting covenant, He will rule us, our *children,* our grandchildren, and on to the end of the world (Ez. 37:24–26). We are not now called to bring forth children to trouble; we are the blessed of the Lord, and our *children* with us (Is. 65:23).

We are the people of the new covenant; we drink the cup of the new covenant. And who is this for? The Spirit is upon us, and His words are in our mouths, and in the mouths of our *children,* and in the mouths of *their* children (Is. 59:21). The mercy of the Lord is from everlasting to those who fear Him, and His righteousness to children's children (Ps. 103:17–18). To think this is automatic, covenant faith or no faith, is absurd— the promise is for those who *believe,* for those who remember His commandments to *do* them. How do we do the works of God? We *believe* Him.

Our Lord's dear mother did not think she was the dead end of all God's promises concerning children. She knew, as a woman of faith, that her womb contained the *beginning* of all God's blessings on all God's children. His mercy is on those who fear Him from generation to generation (Lk. 1:48–50). And in His mercy, He considers my children as His children. After all, the promise is to you and your children (Acts 2:39). These are wonderful words. Christian parents would do well to believe them.

— 11

IN CLOSING

To be understood, almost all of this has to be tasted, not discussed. But as we have tasted it, we have seen that the Lord is good. He has given us His Word, a light in a very dark place, and we have begun to make our way. In no way do we feel that we have in any way arrived. We do not claim to have any special privileged place. We feel the need for ongoing reformation in our own midst as acutely as we ever have. But in our gratitude, we do feel *oriented*. We know which way we are going. We know the nature of the lamp that is lighting our way.

The contemporary Church is in a pathetic condition. The worse things get, the less likely it is that the disaster will be noticed by anyone. Like Laodicea, we have a poor grasp of our true condition. "Because thou sayest, I am rich, and increased with goods, and have need of nothing; and knowest not that thou art wretched, and miserable, and poor, and blind, and naked" (Rev. 3:17).

We sinned our way into this mess together, and we must repent of it together. Our individualism has hidden the nature of our corporate sin from us, but it is a corporate sin nonetheless. American Christians need to start repenting of their strengths and virtues. We need to repent, specifically, of our man-centered gospel and our man-centered response to that gospel. We will soon discover that this repentance must begin in how we worship God. If it begins there, it will soon affect everything else—from the shelves of our local Christian book-shop, to our evangelism, to our observance of the Lord's Day, and so on.

We will come to church expecting the Word to be thundered, not suggested. We will come to the Table weekly in order to be strengthened, fed, and nourished. We will give ourselves to the demanding task of learning hundreds of new (to us) psalms and hymns. And we will learn that the pronouncement of "Ichabod" over the American Church was premature.

---

[7] Meaning, "the glory is departed" (1 Sam. 4:21).

Modernity or medievalism? That is admittedly an odd choice, and it is the topic of this admittedly odd book. But at our place in history it appears to be the only choice before us. History has shown us all the options—nothing is fresh, and everything "new" either fades away or turns out to be just another shadow of modernity. This book aims to answer the question above by defending the impossible—Christian medievalism.

The colors of the essays to follow may not seem to blend together at first glance. They mix such topics as poetry, predestination, and plowshares, with highlights of justification, wine, and lovemaking. We aim to sketch a vision of a whole life and a whole culture, and such things are always a broad landscape of hues. The trick is to realize how these various issues intermingle quite smoothly. We see them as a warm harmony of color, and if the reader grasps the same, then we've accomplished one of our hopes.

Angels in the Architecture
Douglas Jones & Douglas Wilson